W9-CCE-625

AN ALGONQUIAN YEAR

THE YEAR ACCORDING TO THE FULL MOON

Thanks to Michele Rubin, who first proffered the idea of doing this book,
and to my editor, Margaret Raymo, who accepted the idea and saw it through.

Thanks are also given to Joseph Bruchac of the Greenfield Literary Review Center
for his advice during the writing of this text,
and to Susan Stewart of the Pequot Museum Research Center.

Thanks also to my wife, Deborah McCurdy, for her patience in helping me write this book.

This book is dedicated to the descendants of the original Algonquian people.

AN ALGONQUIAN YEAR
THE YEAR ACCORDING TO THE FULL MOON

Written and Illustrated by **MICHAEL McCURDY**

HOUGHTON MIFFLIN COMPANY
BOSTON 2000

INTRODUCTION

Native Americans have long had the custom of assigning descriptive names to each month's full moon. These moon names often differed from one tribe to another, depending on the tribe's geographic location. Using Algonquian moon names as a guide, this book explores an Algonquian year as it would have been lived before the arrival of white settlers. It was a full and busy year, a year that saw a daily round of hunting, fishing, farming, and the struggle for survival.

Algonquians belong to a loosely bound, widespread confederation of tribes that share basic characteristics in language, as well as similar myths and legends. The name Algonquian may have come from the Maliseet word *elakomkwik,* meaning, "They are our relatives or allies," or from the Micmac word *algoomeaking,* interpreted as "They harpoon fish." The French explorer Samuel de Champlain called them *Algoumequin,* while their adversaries, the Iroquois, called them *Adirondack,* or "bark eaters." The Algonquians saw themselves as the "original people." They traced their origins to the "Dawnland," the eastern seaboard, where the sun first rises from the Atlantic Ocean.

An Algonquian Year concentrates on the daily life of Algonquian tribes found in the northeast of what is now Canada and the United States, tribes which included the Micmac, the Abenaki, the Mahican, the Pequot, the Penobscot, and the Wampanoag. Some Algonquian settlements stretched farther west, beyond the eastern seaboard: the Ojibwa (Chippewa) tribe covered about one thousand miles of territory, from southeastern Ontario to the upper Great Lakes, while still farther west, occupying the Great Plains, were Algonquian tribes such as the Blackfoot, Cheyenne, and Arapaho.

There are many full-moon names for every month. While the Crees of northern Canada called January's full moon the Harsh Moon, the Creeks in South Carolina would call the same moon Little Winter Moon. The Penobscots in Maine called the full moon of May the Planting Moon, whereas the Micmacs knew it as the Frog-Croaking Moon. The tribes of the far north had different seasonal habits than of those in more southern areas, and as a result their moon names were different. But regardless of the name of the particular month in which a tribe carried out its daily chores, its labor remained basically the same—a struggle to survive in an often hostile land.

HARD TIMES MOON
JANUARY

January is a harsh month for the winter-bound northern Algonquian people. Deep snow covers the frozen forest, in which wolves, moose, and deer search busily for food. These animals must be hunted down and killed for their meat and fur while the Algonquians are housed in their secluded winter quarters.

Most Algonquians in the Northeast live in small clusters of dome-shaped wigwams. These dwellings are built in secluded inland valleys, sheltered as much as possible from the harsh winter winds. Each wigwam is made from saplings that are lashed together with cedar or basswood fibers and covered with bark from elm, walnut, or birch trees. Sometimes mats made from woven corn husks and cattail stalks are used as well. An animal skin, draped over the wigwam's opening, is used as a door. A hole at the top allows smoke to escape. Some Algonquians build a fence of sharpened stakes around their little village of wigwams for protection from enemies.

Each wigwam houses one family or two related families who have their own space in the wigwam. The family members sleep on platforms, covered with skins or mats, that are built against the wigwam's walls. An open fire burns constantly, over which simmers a stew from which family members feed whenever they are hungry. Although the fire provides some light and heat, wigwams are often cold, smoky, and congested inside. During this difficult month, hunters track the white-tailed deer and giant moose in the snowy woods in a continual search for food.

SNOW BLINDER MOON
FEBRUARY

February is a time of heavy snow and winds that whistle through the forests, often blinding the Algonquian hunters. The threat of starvation is very real for these northern tribes. The last harvest's stored grains, dried meat, and smoked fish will soon be used up.

Algonquian hunting families spend part of the winter on the trail in the hunting grounds, far from their central villages. They set up small wigwams while tracking game in the winter forest. After a successful hunt, everybody helps skin the animal and dry its meat. The hunters always give thanks to the spirit that lived within the animal they have killed. Once the hunters have enough meat, the men, women, and older children carry it in pieces on their backs or on sleds and return to the main village. Snowshoes make the difficult work of winter travel a little easier as the families journey over the deep, narrow trails.

In the villages, the children are growing restless. They long to roam the woodlands again, but they must wait until the terrain is free of its snow pack. Soon the Frost Spirit will walk among the forest trees, tapping them with its hammer and breaking the snow and ice from their bent boughs. It will be the first sign of the spring thaw.

SAP MOON
MARCH

Life seems to stir again in the northeastern lands. With great anticipation, the Algonquians wait for the sap to rise in the trees. While there is still snow on the ground, the women and children gather in their sugar camps to collect sap from several different kinds of trees, including box elder, walnut, hickory, birch, and black cherry. The sweetest sap of all, though, comes from the sugar maple.

There is a carnival-like atmosphere as the women use tomahawks to cut deep slashes in the bark of the maple trees. They then attach a twig or flat stick to each tree at the bottom of the slash, allowing the sap to drip slowly down the twig and into tightly made buckets of birch bark, which are carefully folded in such a way as to not lose a single drop of the sap. The prized liquid is then poured into hollowed-out logs, into which red-hot stones are dropped in order to bring the sap to a boil. More stones are added until most of the sap's water has turned to steam and disappeared, leaving behind a thick, sweet syrup. Indian children pour a little of the syrup on the snow, creating a kind of sugar candy.

According to legend, Algonquians learned to gather maple sap by watching gray squirrels gnaw the bark of maple trees and lick the juice that oozed from the tree. The Algonquian tribes will one day show the white settlers how to make maple syrup.

SPEARFISH MOON
APRIL

Fish are plentiful again in rivers and lakes. The Abenakis and Micmacs fish for smelt, salmon, bass, and sturgeon. Sometimes Micmacs of the north venture into the ocean to hunt for porpoises and even whales—as do the more southern Algonquians, such as the Montauks, Wampanoags, and Shinnecocks. On the river they call Mahicanituk, which will someday be called the Hudson River, the Mahicans catch herring and shad while the Lenapes harvest the same fish from the Delaware River.

The fishermen use wooden spears, gaffs, and dip nets to catch their prey. During the night, the light from their torches lures fish into the nets. Fences called *weirs,* made of latticework or closely set poles, are often set across streams or at the outlets of lakes. When fish try to pass through the narrow opening of a weir, they are easily caught. Some weirs are built in saltwater harbors: fish swim over the fence during high tide and are trapped when the tide goes out. Some of the catch is eaten right away and the rest is smoked for use during the long winter months to come.

PLANTING MOON
MAY

Some northern Algonquian tribes now migrate in small family groups to more fertile and easily tilled lands near rivers, lakes, or the ocean. There they build more portable wigwams. These small wigwams, with their open doors always facing east toward the rising sun, usually hold only one family.

Both men and women break the spring soil in the fields with hoes made of flat stones. Later, when they are weeding, they use hoes made of wood, large clamshells, or the shoulder blades of deer and bear. The women and children plant seeds by dropping kernels of corn in carefully spaced hills of earth. Beans are planted next to the corn so the bean plant will grow upward on the cornstalk. Squashes are planted between the corn and beans. Gourds are grown too, and when harvested are hollowed out. Dried, they become vessels for carrying water and food.

If their gardens produce abundant crops, families usually remain in the same location until the fall. If not, they move their villages to find better farmland. Those who decide to move take the bark coverings and fiber ropes from the wigwams with them, leaving behind the sapling frame.

STRAWBERRY MOON
JUNE

Algonquian tribes love wild strawberries. They call the juicy red fruit "grassberries." It is said that these red berries ripen evenly because the mythical Mikumwesu, or "Little People," come to the strawberry patches at night to water them and turn them over with their tiny hands.

When ripe, the wild berries are harvested by old women and children, who sit on the warm ground and pluck the delicate fruit with great care. The berries are placed into baskets for everyone to share. Not all the strawberries that the Algonquians enjoy are wild, for they also plant and harvest their favorite fruit in great abundance in areas to which they return every year. Other berries are plentiful as well, such as thimbleberries, blackberries, shadberries, raspberries, and elderberries. All grow in natural clearings, or in fields that the Algonquians allow to lie fallow between harvest years.

During this month, the women and children continue to cultivate the rich soil around the corn, which is growing taller with every passing week. This is a good time for Algonquian families. Fresh food is growing in their fields and gardens, and there is a plentiful supply of fish in the rivers and lakes.

RIPENING MOON
JULY

July, with its frequent thunderstorms, is the time of ripening crops. Corn, the Indians' most precious food, has now grown much taller. The gardens still need constant attention, for weeds must not choke the growing fruits and vegetables. Even the children are especially busy during the month of the ripening moon: they help the women pull weeds and they chase away the many birds that are eager to eat the valuable crop. Often, scaffolds are built from which women and children scare away the attacking birds.

The men spend much time tending their tobacco plants in special gardens that are set apart from the food crops. The smoked leaf of the tobacco plant plays an important role in the lives of the eastern tribes. The rising smoke from a pipe is visible evidence of the Algonquians' desire to contact the spirit powers above. By smoking a pipe, an Indian asks for support from the spirit powers and demonstrates his commitment to those spirits.

During these summer months, the coastal tribes fish the ocean and collect shellfish, which are in great abundance. Soft-shell crabs, as well as the hard-shell clams called quahogs, are gathered by the Wampanoags along the coast of Massachusetts. Lobsters are caught, too, but these strange creatures are not eaten—they are used only as bait for catching fish.

GREEN CORN MOON
AUGUST

The ripened corn is now ready to eat. It is picked by everyone, including mothers who work in the fields while their babies, bound on cradleboards, are hung on nearby tree branches. To celebrate the corn harvest, families perform thanksgiving ceremonies dressed in specially decorated clothing. Algonquian children find other uses for corn: they make their own corn-husk dolls.

During the summer months, games are a favorite pastime. Throwing darts made from the stems of cattail plants and goose or swan feathers, swatting wooden or stone balls with sticks, and running long footraces are popular activities. So, too, is the game that we now call lacrosse.

But there are always chores that need to be done. The women make baskets from birch bark. They also use tough deerskin to create the clothes needed for the winter. The hides are first scraped of fat and flesh and the hair is removed. Then the skins are soaked in oil and washed. Next they are pulled and stretched to soften them, and finally they are smoked at a smudge fire. Smoking will help the skins last a long time.

HARVEST MOON
SEPTEMBER

It is now harvest time for most of the northeastern Algonquian tribes. Any surplus of dried corn is stored snugly in baskets, to be placed within well-covered underground cellars lined with birch bark. The last of the ripened vegetables are hung up to dry, and meat is cut into thin strips and smoked. Fish is hung on racks over slow-burning, smoky fires.

The difficult and uncertain winter months lie ahead, and a return to winter quarters will come soon. Algonquians hold a celebration to give thanks to the spirits and to the Creator for a good harvest. But there is never enough stored food to meet the tribe's needs until spring. Hunters must prepare to track game during the coming winter. They spend time making arrowheads, sharpening stone spear blades, and repairing canoes and bows. Though times may become difficult, Algonquian families are always generous, sharing their food with anyone who comes by. They know that they, too, might someday be hungry and in need of another's generosity.

HUNTER'S MOON
OCTOBER

Since the spring and summer, the men of the village have been taking note of where deer gather to feed. After harvest time, when the forest's leaf cover has thinned out, the hunters leave their villages. They travel alone or in small groups to hunt deer, moose, elk, or bear—sometimes covering twenty miles in one day. At times, entire families spend weeks away from the village in their bark-covered hunting shelters. They set traps and snares to catch animals. These are checked daily, often by the tribe's women and children.

Some families gather in large groups for the deer hunt. They may use the *hedge drive*— a large, funnel-shaped fence made of bushes and stakes. The deer are driven from the broad opening of the funnel toward the narrow end, where other hunters are waiting with bows, arrows, and spears. Algonquians sometimes burn hunting areas to encourage tender new grass, which invites deer to feed where they can be easily killed.

It might take hunters a couple of days to carry a deer or moose back to the village. The animal's hide will be used for clothing, its bones and antlers for tools. Wolves, foxes, and wildcats are also hunted—not for food, but for the warm skins they will provide for the cold winter ahead. Bears are a good source of meat and fur. Bear grease may be used for cooking and for protection against the sun, insects, and the cold. For the Micmacs, bear grease even serves as an occasional snack, once it is sweetened with sassafras or slippery-elm bark.

BEAVER MOON
NOVEMBER

The Abenakis of northern New England have left their summer villages to go off in small groups for the winter, stalking deer and moose in the interior woodlands. But the families of southern New England tribes often leave their summer camps to return to central villages deeper in the forest, where they settle in for a long winter. November is cloudy and cold. Winter's teeth begin to show as ponds, bogs, swamps, and lakes freeze over.

Beaver, fattened by their summer diet of greens, prepare to spend the winter snug in their lodges. Algonquians set traps for the beaver before solid ice makes it more difficult to capture them. Beaver tail, cooked in bear grease, is a delicacy served at Algonquian feasts, and sharp beaver teeth make excellent cutting edges for tools. Beaver pelts are valued as warm clothing. Someday, when the European settlers arrive, the pelts will be traded for the white man's goods.

TOMCOD MOON
DECEMBER

For the Micmacs living in what someday will be called New Brunswick, each full moon brings with it a different hunt. In this northern maritime land, the rocky earth is too hard for hoeing and digging, and the growing season is short. Farming that requires the use of bone, wood, and shell tools is of little use here. As a result, the Micmac must hunt and fish year-round for their food. In January they will hunt seal, in March they will fish for smelt, and in April they will hunt the returning geese. September is eel-hunting time, while in October the Micmacs seek out beaver and elk. But for now, the month of December brings the annual fishing for tomcod.

Micmac fishermen drop fish lines with bone hooks through holes cut in the ice, hoping to catch the small saltwater fish as they swim quickly below them. It is very cold now on the ice, and the fisherman feel the bite of the northern winds as they lower their hooks and hope for a catch.

The pleasant summer activities are long past as the Algonquians settle in for the long, cold winter.

BIBLIOGRAPHY

Algonquians of the East Coast. Alexandria, Va.: Time-Life Books, 1995.

Calloway, Colin G. *The Abenaki.* New York: Chelsea House, 1989.

Hoxie, Frederick E., ed. *Encyclopedia of North American Indians.* Boston: Houghton Mifflin, 1996.

Siegel, Beatrice. *Indians of the Northeast Woodlands.* New York: Walker, 1992.

Weinstein-Farson, Laurie. *The Wampanoag.* New York: Chelsea House, 1989.

www.hmco.com/trade

The text of this book is set in Berthold Garamond.
The illustrations are scratchboard.

Library of Congress Cataloging-in-Publication Data
McCurdy, Michael.
An Algonquian year : the year according to the full moon / Michael McCurdy.
p.   cm.
Includes bibliographical references.
Summary: Describes the life of the Algonquian Indians, month by month,
as it would have been before the arrival of white settlers.
ISBN 0-618-00705-9
1. Algonquian Indians – Juvenile literature. [1. Algonquian Indians.
2. Indians of North America.] I. Title
E99.A35 M364   2000
973'.04973 – dc21
99-087157

Manufactured in the United States of America
WOZ 10 9 8 7 6 5 4 3 2 1

973   McCurdy, Michael.
MCC
           An Algonquian year.

                                    YPVE58240

$15.00

DATE			

BAKER & TAYLOR